ECOLOGY
OF THE
AFTERLIFE

ICONES ANIMALIUM ET PLANTARUM

ISBN 978-1-7354839-2-4

Split Rock Press is dedicated to publishing eco-friendly books that explore place, environment, and the relationship between humans and the natural world. Visit us online at www.splitrockreview.org/press.

Environmental consciousness is important to us. This book is printed with chlorine-free ink and acid-free paper stock supplied by a Forest Stewardship Council certified provider. The paper stock is made from 30% post-consumer waste recycled material.

ECOLOGY
OF THE
AFTERLIFE

ICONES ANIMALIUM ET PLANTARUM

poems & illustrations by

NATHAN MANLEY

Split Rock Press
Washburn, WI
2021

For Kirstie

*Fecit autem haec omnia Deus in usum hominis, ut serviant aut subjuciantur
ei omnia, sine natura iussu Dei perpetuo, ut elementa, caeli, et corpora
inanima.*

God made all these, the animals, for the use of Man, that all should
serve him or be brought by him under the yoke—without Nature to be
commanded by God everlasting—just as He made the elements, the
heavens, and even lifeless objects.

— Conrad Gesner, *Icones animalium* (1560)

TABLE OF CONTENTS

Vanvoorstia bennettiana
"Bennett's seaweed"

To begin, the sea laid lungless, heaving
great and imperturbable vacancies
at any horizon it should fathom.
Spirits moved upon the deep; thus kingdoms
bloomed and slithered, flourished at the mercies
of current—hidden, the god's hand grieving

plenitude at its own touch. Bloodred wings
unfolded, filiform, across the gloom
and tended skyward: sun-flutter, sun-creel,
sunset. Steamships, unzippering the real,
split the wriggling oceans open: this loom
from which the Earth made of itself each thing,

small, grief-worthy: this shadow-wearied fan,
light-thriving, starved where once a world began.   – c. 1884

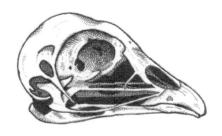

Tympanuchus cupido cupido
"Heath hen"

It is unusual to see a Heath Hen perched in a tree . . .
[b]ut a bird bereft of all its companions might well
be expected to do that which is unusual.
  — Alfred O. Gross, *The Heath Hen Census for 1929*

Islands within islands within islands.

Ocean-fold: old Atlantic humps its back,
recumbent, loops blue statics up the strand,
shoreline-spool. Wind, far off and chatter-blent,
dwindling among scrub oaks. The remnant flock
persists. Evening preens itself, approaching

fields that boom with otherworldly musicks
as of old. A morning star un-sutures
the dark, enough to write by—a trickling
light: another, outer island.
                    A fire.
A hard winter and a flight of goshawks.

Time, that shining machine, uncoils its chain
and drops the hour ponderously, subtle
as a gilt cylinder.
                    The birds return
by morning. Bright sun ascendant, lurching:
a poverty. Summer flares and is lost.

Hunkered in a blind of thatch-grass, they leer

– 1907: seventy-seven, still singing.

– 1916: again, thousands.

– May 12th, 1916: fifty pairs, perhaps;
      a male remainder.

– 1923: twenty-eight.

– 1927: thirteen, two female;
      by fall, only seven.

and photograph the sedge; scientists mark
the clockwork toll of disappearances.
Three, then two—   – April, 1928
                    the all-anticipated
one.   – December 8th, 1928

    This last sputters above the bramble,
lights upon a bough of oak, plumage sprung—
drawerful of knives—at once inclines its throat,
swollen and dawn-colored. Singing: each note
an island sinking in the sea-swept air.   – Spring, 1929

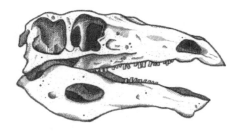

Stegosaurus stenops
"Roofed lizard"

Reverence first gave rise to reverie,
one Hereafter's tropic-colored splendor,
in the picture-book hagiographies
of dinosaurs and prehistoric beasts,
plucked from low shelves in my mother's study.
I learned to read by naming them, these saints
of ancient Earth: monstrous, un-answering
as angels in the tangerine lamplight
that pooled beside her desk.
                              Saint *smilodon*
of the puncture wound, of tooth and run blood,
martyred in a tar pit . . . and our Lady,
plesiosaurus, of the wrenching tide,
of gracile neck, reputed now to scrawl
plumes of silt in the bellies of deep lakes.
Best of all, I loved old *stegosaurus,*
who bore bright petals on his back, planted
in the landscapes of the late Jurassic
like a flower, bulbous, otherworldly,
alive to the exalted pointlessness
of architecture: lovely for my sake.

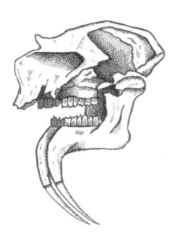

Deinotherium giganteum
"Terrible beast"

Having plumbed the esoteric anchor
of its mouth, ivory that struck its roots
in hell or slipped them in a famished past
grown depth-dark and equal to it, some Greek,
having thumbed the Cretan soil deftly out
the orbits of the bone and planted there
his mythic nerve, great glint and glowering
of the cyclops' eye—he must have turned it,
probing the cloisters of its phantom flesh,
where membranous folds of meat once glistened
and parsed the electrochemical flood,
drop by indissoluble drop, and knew
the world as it's known, perhaps, even now
by hidden caves, conjuring slow crystals
from the lime-smart damp: pretty minerals,
they must sparkle like the Pleistocene light
of the sky's sown field, cartographer's stars
that startle and hale us into the night.

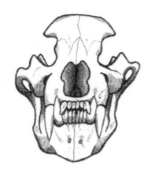

Ursus arctos crowtheri
"Atlas bear"

Down among the sunken arcades, the sky
flutes blue lightenings across the breakage,
through the shattered ribs of colonnades. Dusk
and the ruin blooms like a scavenged corpse.

Memory and spectacle and the pluck
of my heart at its impotent magicks,
its vain pursuit of the bear mosaicked
in the buried floor—a living likeness

shut in the febrile hulls of Roman ships,
a ravening trafficked in the city,
set and glutted on grim resignations
of flesh: *damnatio ad bestias.*

Relict populations pocked the Atlas
as the long cascades of empire swallowed
even the underworld's unshining pools.
The last specimen was shot, sketched, and skinned

in the sprawling reign of Victoria,   – 1841
then named. The world's a museum of these
small and thoughtless cruelties, the night's spell
breaking, a broken temple on the hill.

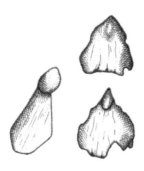

Picaea critchfieldii
"Critchfield's spruce"

Cowed against the patient, stone-deep scrimshaw
of northern glaciers, the forest once struck
its ragged frontiers with the scope and pluck
of a Roman legion—damned, at length drawn

to meet a Pharsalus or an Actium
the scripts of silt and pollen in our lakes
obscure; for the unpitiable sake
of God, the water wastes its cadmium

toward some mystery in what's reflected
there. For the glassy scientific eye
marks particles, but cannot patternize
the ghost by which they fell, uncollected

out of life: the spirit creeping starwise
through a lattice, the seedwing locked in ice.

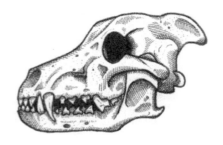

Canis dirus
"Dire wolf"

Gehenna's iridescent lips open
into asphalt seeps, slow spume in black lakes
spattered at La Brea—no sound of wolves
which, dredged from the technician-harrowed pits,
un-catalogue these ossuaries. Dark
with tar and contemplated by it, bone
by bone, another wolf emerges, slick
as an elision, from the muddled pack—
its congregated greed extinguished, drowned
at a rotten font of mammoth flesh.

But for all the damaged dead, one woman.   – 1914
One dog. Redeemed of the ten-thousand
trenchant teeth that hell's no longer full of,
a spooling, incoherent strand of light
frets its questions, prismatic on the deep.

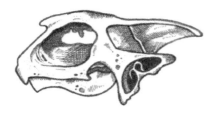

Cylindraspis vosmaeri
"Saddle-backed Rodriguez giant tortoise" [1]

We have eaten Eden. Spill'd the Palm Wines
of Paradise from a Gash once savag'd
and guzzl'd at its Root. By Hook and Barb
we have pierc'd the Flesh, wrench'd the work-worn Ends
of Harping Iron—dredg'd resplendent Eels,
writhing, from the crystal Burn. We have gone
above a hundred flightless Paces o'er
Fields upon the teeming Backs of Turtles;
treading Air, lo, they cannot right themselves
once upturn'd by dint of Arms or Levers.
Their soft Meat smacks of Mutton, tho the Bones,
throwaways, crack massy and marrowless.

Thus we slept, full-bellied, at the Banyan's Foot
and dreamt of Shells—star-hearted, collapsing
heedless of our secret Hells; thence comes Fire
in dark Trees, wither'd of unslak'd Desire.

---

[1] In the spring of 1691, François Leguat, a Huguenot and ship's naturalist, was marooned on Rodriguez during a voyage to reconnoiter the Mascarene Islands off the eastern coast of Madagascar. Following the eventual escape of Leguat and his crew to nearby Mauritius, Leguat penned a memoir of the incident, published decades later in 1708. This book, *Voyage et avantures de François Leguat et de ses compagnons, en deux isles désertes des Indes orientales*, is remarkable for its descriptions of several megafaunal species since driven to extinction by human contact. Among these were the Rodriguez solitaire, a large flightless bird, and two species of tortoise.

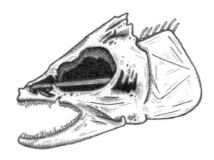

Salvelinus agassizii
"Silver trout"

Nacreous sheen of the under-scale, splayed
at a blade's tip.
                    Limp silver the body
shucked, spills thence into the puckered coin purse
of the hand.
                    Rasp to sequin and blood-kiss.

You, rapt in the rude scholarship of it,
count the scales, mucous-slick, across your palm,
biding the summer with a mute interest.   – c. 1930

From the cemetery-facing window
where I, biding mine, invent the past,
I trace your lapse into divination:

the hieroglyphic gleam of the ruin
you parse, untranslatably.
                    The mirror
of Monadnock Lake,
            my paternoster.

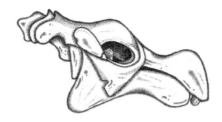

Hydrodamalis gigas
"Steller's sea cow"

. . . often it was my wont to get milk in large quantities
from dead ones in the same way as from cows.
  — Georg Wilhelm Steller, *de Bestiis Marinis* (1751)

Bark-skinned and buoyant as a rotten log,
the leviathan of Bering Island
was first hauled, wrenchingly, by shipwrecked men
to shore—who filleted and flayed its corpse   – 1742

upon the beach. Steller cut the details
knife-wise: one black, prevaricating eye,
blinking in the sleep of which his own gleamed,
or seemed to, taken at any angle.

What remained of the hide inviolate
when the grim labor of the cudgels slowed
and slackened to a pant, they peeled away—
scraps, fit only for belts and for boot soles.

The creature's rich, unspoiled fat, sun-softened
and rendered, burned smokelessly, was almost
sweet-scented, though it tended to impart
certain haunted inflections to the light

Steller wrote by, despoiling the body's
hidden rooms, flesh-ensconced machineries,
the deep, arborescent architectures

of blood and sensation—*de anima*;
for, shooing seagulls from the days-dead thing,
he marked the lone and listless silhouette
of a bull, like a felled tree, as it bobbed
along the rain-frothed shoal, holding vigil.

The descendants of this expedition
met with an isle of mysterious bones: – c. 1820
relics to be collected and pedaled
at far harbors as mermaid ivory.

    Vest, not unselfishly, a devotion
    in this. That life might seek its quiet end,
    lapped at the leisure of the long-tailed sea,
    in use. Pick me over. Clean me out, Lord.

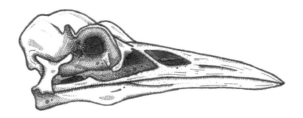

Nycticorax olsoni
"Ascension night heron"

A florid holography, the seabirds
turning, ink-dark and mutable as rain,
splutters of Ascension-blue: Isle of Gyres
some sailor once improbably mistook
for the mind of a god, a Poseidon-
of-the-South-Atlantic's all-composing
thought, by votive flock lighted and lighting.

Small deaths diminished him.
                        Rat-black shadows
cast of men outlived their masters, teeming
shoreward, ship-borne. The island laid its feast
for vermin.
            A familiar story.

From what aery contemplations welter
on the wing-troubled cliffs, we cannot cull
the heron's song, nor figure the flourish
it swept across the moon's blind eye, haunting
seawater's pale break like a history.

Silphium
"Laserwort" [2]

First flower, still silvering on the face
of the tarnished coin—Cyrenaican,   – c. 260 BCE
smooth as a gullet stone; that pelican,
Time, disgorging throatfuls it displaces

from the tide-wracked bed of a sleeping age.
Resin of the desiccated root, balm
of the uncultivable bloom last palmed
by the ailing emperor on a page   – c. 63 CE

in Pliny's histories—an absence still
un-cicatrized upon the living stalk
of medicine, this art; the augur's flock
now clicks its claws on empty air and spills

its shadows like a language: first flower,
icon of the unburiable hour.

---

[2] Some scholars have identified *silphium* (also, *laserpitium*) as the first species extinction to appear in the historical record. Laser, a *silphium* extract lauded by Mediterranean peoples for its medicinal qualities, was highly prized and much traded in antiquity. By the third century BCE, laser had become the chief export of Cyrenaica (modern Libya), a region in which *silphium* grew abundantly in the wild. According to Pliny the Elder, the last known stalk of *silphium* was presented four centuries later to the Roman emperor Nero as a curiosity. The species taxon of *silphium* has not been definitely identified.

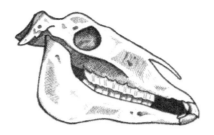

Equus ferus ferus
"Tarpan"

An empire of horses, worn muslin-thin
down the Scythian steppe, came to tatters
at the century's edge—let drop, perhaps,
its last raveled thread at the woodland source
of Hypanis, where Herodotus dreamed
a pale herd, grazing.
                    The last wild tarpan
    shattered itself down the base of a scarp,
    uncaptured, at Askania-Nova.   – 1879

    Died with a bit in its mouth and buckled,
    mouse-grey in the bloodied dust of a zoo
    at Moscow.   – 1887
                    At Munich in the same year,
    or in Poland.

                    Persisted quietly
    into a late decline at the estate
    near Mirgorod—disconsolate stallion,
    old dun coat the color of withered grass.   – 1919

History treats of the tarpan's absence
as nightmare treats of the body, of mine:
the missing teeth, the odd finger severed
and furtively stashed in a dresser drawer.
This interminable hunger after,
so deep it becomes a kind of knowledge.

Aepyornis maximus
"Elephant bird"

On the thrilling breath of Scheherazade
borne into a kind of afterlife, wings
still ink their fathoms down the yellowed page
in merchants' memoirs: tale of golden plume
plucked of hidden empires, nestled precious
among gemstones in a gut-warm pocket
and ported, twinkling dimly toward Venice.

Eagle of supernatural span—no,
stunted as an ostrich, idiot-bird.

A dull shell thick as a Spanish dollar,
observes the surgeon of a trade ship, moored
in 1848 at the far port
of Tuléar; Madagascan natives
offer up the globe of a hollowed egg
to be filled with rum. Ornaments and bowls
cup vanished embryos, the past's plenty.

From the Neolithic hearth, black fragments
betray butchery and lineage. For,
by adze-bite and bone shard we know they gorged
on marrows, our fathers—the ghost eaters.

Glaucopsyche xerces
"Xerces blue"

A Babylon above the dunes, dazzling
the sky to tiles in its spires of glasswork,
skeleton-steel—by its cells, the city
also dreams of ordering an ocean
to quell the all-dilapidating blue,
flatten, stanch it to a depthless silver
salt-air licks the face of, but cannot eat.

Bright wings line the lepidopterist's drawer,
opalescent in the light and silent:
the twentieth century's chrome-hard glint.   – 1941
All the brittle bodies, once collected,
of the country's rarest extant species
might amount to three pounds, hardly deadweight—
after-shape held in the unburdened hand.

Still, aloft our many-mirrored empire
of erasures, above the crimson bridge,
some wingèd thing, fog-lost, is fluttering.

Incilius periglenes
"Golden toad"

An Age of Rain passed, tadpole-filigreed,
upon the clouded mountain.
                              Having lost
his love from its beginning, young Sky pined
after the Earth and made thus of himself
a vast and perpetual fog, brooding
about the braided sprigs and limbs of trees
like a spectral hand, spangling canopies
by the flicker and weave of white-hot tongue—
raptures of electric flame.
                              Hard rains fell
and took Earth's shape among the roots. Insects
spawned like curious beadworks, enameled
half-spheres spun of fog-lit air. Scuttling things
abounded, lithe and thousand-leggèd forms,
clicking in the underwood. Mud-glum, May
gave rise to comely toads—the auric shine
of them, leaping like automata, strange
and dextrously wrought, as if from the finger
of some happy horologist: goldsmith
fit to fire unearthly admirations.

When lesser gods, wily and covetous,
looked upon an Earth thus ornamented,
they took of her blushing clays and made men
who could not love them. Of tempered metals,
men fashioned furnaces to which each fed
his varicolored misery—thinned it
to a blackish cloud, stench of sweat and soot.

The last of all the gilded toads, sighted
a road grown mossy and sunless, fled   – Spring, 1989
from wincing Sky, in whom the long rains ceased.

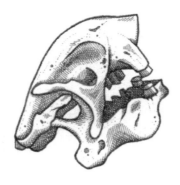

Megalonyx jeffersonii
"Jefferson's ground sloth"

What is become of the great-claw? In the present interior
of our continent there is surely space and range enough for
elephants and lions... and for mammoths and megalonyxes
who may subsist there.

— Thomas Jefferson, *Transactions of the American Philosophical Society* (1797)

The bones exist. Therefore, the animal.
And the undiscovered world still burning
its pluralities behind the curtain
of the backcountry, in the mouths of men
returning tall tales and contradictions
on campfired tongues, where the forests empty
westward into an alien landscape
of the Unknown-but-knowable.
                                        Nature,
clawed in kind, cuts her circuits endlessly
beneath us.
                         In 1770,
a hunter, hastened by the sound of bells
about a distant bridle, scenting thieves,
gave chase through grot and thicket, finally
descrying entrails, such oozing half-moons
as compassed the poor colt's belly, blood strung
up the tangled trees—a sorry carcass.
Even the hounds were still.

Jefferson's claw,
classed by Cuvier, benign, split in hunger
only earth, crooked thence from it only roots
and tubers, bushelfuls of which sustained
the shaggy tower of an ancient sloth.
All this picked of a remnant spine, its nest
of broken rings, the fossil hook.
                                    Thus comes
each by turns to grief. Life's less cruelty
than accumulation, buried wreckage:
a winter at the end of everything.

— Recherches sur les os
sements fossils de
quadrupèdes, 1812

Viola cryana
"Cry violet"

By the gravedigger's mute geometry
a quarry deepens in the limestone hills,
sculpting air along the perfect angles
of its absences. A bucket dangles
from the backhoe's gathered arm, steel sleep-stilled
and silvered. By the creeping psaltery

of suns plucked on the underside of Earth,
green things feed on night's interposition
and suckle water from the graveled stones.
To subtler climes, the meadow's ghost is flown;
thus, this flower purples in my vision—
wilts, the past at its unbridgeable berth,

into a Latin-captioned photograph,
the archive-silence of the epitaph.   – c. 1927

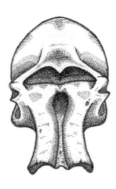

Mammut americanum/Mammuthus columbi
"American mastodon/Columbian mammoth"

Out of the winter of another world
they loomed, draped along iron armatures
a raptured boy could scarcely distinguish
from bone, mounted in a Hall of Giants,
where, far from the prairie of my childhood
(the island of our town against the wild;
pronghorn and grouse at the outskirts), I stood
with my parents in the old museum,
its atria many-windowed, alive
with the cathedral's atomizing light
and long consecrated to the breathless
worship of monsters. O, how I loved them,
and learned their strange taxonomies, and knew
the mammoth by the calligraphic curve
of its tusk, and so, too, the mastodon
by the ghostly, elephantine echoes
of its song—
                              but this makes poor elegy,
for the mammoth and the pronghorn are gone,
the past, so thoroughly imagined
that one returns with frequency and ease,
and longs for grieflessness, for the many
misplaced sureties of boyhood—the wild,
blue height of heaven: Sunday-safe, waiting.
If only you could steel your heart and climb.

Melanoplus spretus
"Rocky Mountain locust"

And they shall cover the face of the earth, that one
cannot be able to see the earth...and shall eat every
tree which groweth for you out of the field: And they
shall fill thy houses and the houses of all thy servants . . .
   — Exodus 10:5-6 (KJV)

Sun-shuttering abundance, a music
deepened to machine, wind-sprung and thrumming
at the edges of everything. The sum
of all the scattered signals spindling out
from stars, the noise coincident in light
that animates the patchwork silences
of sky between radios, sounds in this.

The insects gnashed and spat, set listeners
ablaze with the million crackling statics
of their jaws.
              From the porch, you noted first
the futile scent of kerosene, shining
in a ditch—lantern cracked and crimson-hulled—
when, ears attuned to the swarming field, you
heard human voices in it, dissolving
with the landscape: fence posts and hung linen,
the painted handle of your mother's spade.   – 1875

Once your labor's eaten to its shadows,
you'll kneel in moonscapes, this Grand Deletion,
and claw theodicies from knits of root.

30

Megaloceros giganteus
"Irish elk"

Like the sail of a phantom galleon,
you light your sylvan course—St. Elmo's fire
to green the marvel of your eyes, met here,
as headlights scatter in black trees, with mine,
fleshly through the moving glass and searching
an Earth you could not recognize: glaciers
spent, mere spirit; some many-million mouths
healed over with hornet-comb and moss; seas
broad-pathed and glooming where the landscapes end.

And yet I sketch the mizzenmast of you,
now dreaming down the wood, as if, grace-like,
you'd ferry us all to the worlds we've hoped for.

BIBLIOGRAPHY

Conservatoire Botanique National Du Bassin Parisien, "Violette de Cry," Bassin Parisien, accessed November 19, 2020. http://cbnbp.mnhn.fr/cbnbp/especeAction.do?action=fiche&cdNom=129545

Cuvier, Georges, *Recherches sur les ossements fossiles de quadrupèdes* (Paris: Deterville, 1812).

Department of Agriculture, Water and the Environment, "Vanvoorstia bennettiana (Bennett's Seaweed), a marine red alga," Australian Government, accessed November 19, 2020. http://www.environment.gov.au/biodiversity/threatened/conservation-advices/vanvoorstia-bennettiana

Epstein, H., "The Origin of the Domesticated Animals of Africa," *Journal of Mammalogy* 54, no. 1 (April 1973): 574.

Gesner, Conrad, *Icones Animalium,* 2nd ed. (Zurich: Christof Froshover, 1560) 3.

Godolphin, Francis R.B., ed., *The Greek Historians* (London: Random House, Inc. 1970) 135.

Gross, Alfred O., "The Heath Hen Census for 1929," *The Wilson Bulletin* 41, no. 2 (June 1929): 67, 71.

Gross, Alfred O., "The Last Heath Hen," *The Scientific Monthly* 32, no. 4 (April 1931): 382, 383.

Haddad, Nick, "A Sliver of Creation," chap. 1 in *The Last Butterflies* (Princeton: Princeton University Press, 2019) 2, 15.

Jackson, Stephen T. and Chengyu Weng, "Late Quaternary extinction of a tree species in eastern North America," *PNAS* 96, No. 24 (November 1999): 13847, 13851-52.

Jardine, William, *Contributions to Ornithology* (London: Samuel Highley, 1848) 125.

Jefferson, Thomas, "A memoir on the Discovery of certain bones of a quadruped of the Clawed Kind in the Western Parts of Virginia," in *Transactions of the American Philosophical Society*, Vol. 4 (Philadelphia: Thomas Dobson, 1799) 307, 310.

Johnston, H.H., "African Bear," in *Great and Small Game of Africa* (London: Roland Ward, LTD.,1899) 606.

Jones, Ryan Tucker, "A 'Havock Made among Them': Animals, Empire and Extinction in the Russian North Pacific," *Environmental History* 16, no. 4 (October 2011): 593.

Leguat, François, *The Voyage of François Leguat,* Vol. 1, ed. Pasfield Oliver (London: The Hakluyt Society, 1891) 61, 70-72.

Ley, William, "Scheherazade's Island," *Galaxy Magazine,* August 1966, 45-55.

Lydekker, R., *The Horse and Its Relatives* (London: George Allen & Company, Ltd., 1912).

Mayor, Adrienne, *The First Fossil Hunters: Dinosaurs, Mammoths, and Myth in Greek and Roman Times* (Princeton: Princeton University Press, 2011).

Miller, Robert R. et al., "Extinctions of North American Fishes During the Past Century," *Fisheries* 14, no. 6 (November – December 1989): 24-25.

Ochoa-Ochoa, Leticia M. et al., "The Demise of the Golden Toad and the Creation of a Climate Change Icon Species," *Conservation and Society* 11, no. 3 (2013): 291-92.

Pannell, James H., "The Heath Hen," *Science* 98, no. 2538 (August 1943): 174.

Parejko, Ken, "Pliny the Elder's Silphium: First Recorded Species Extinction," *Conservation Biology* 17, no. 3 (June 2003) 925.

Pliny the Elder, *The Natural History,* Book XIX, chap. 15 (London: Taylor and Francis, 1855). http://data.perseus.org/citations/urn:cts:latinLit:phi0978.phi001.perseus-eng1:19.15

R.L. Reynolds, "Domestic dog associated with human remains at Rancho La Brea" (Los Angeles: Bulletin, Southern California Academy of Sciences, 1985), 76-85.

Savage, Jay M., "An Extraordinary New Toad from Costa Rica," *Revista de BiologíaTropical* 50, no. 2 (June 2002). https://www.scielo.sa.cr/scielo.php?pid=S0034774420020002000033&script=sci_arttext&tlng=en

Schlebecker, John T., "Grasshoppers in American Agricultural History," *Agricultural History* 27, no. 3 (July 1953): 86.

Shapiro, Arthur M., "Coppers, Hairstreaks, Blues, and Metalmarks—The Gossamer-winged Butterflies," in *Field Guide to Butterflies of the San Francisco Bay and Sacramento Valley Regions* (Berkeley: University of California Press, 2007) 149.

Shaw, Christopher A. and James P. Quinn, "Rancho La Brea: A Look at Coastal Southern California's Past," *California Geology* 39, no. 6 (June 1986): 130.

Steller, Georg Wilhelm, *De Bestiis Marinis*, trans. Walter Miller and Jennie Emmerson Miller (St. Petersburg: Typia Academiae Scientiarum, 1751; Lincoln: University of Nebraska, 2011) 26, 45, 46-47.

Steller, Gerog Wilhelm, *Journal of a Voyage with Bering*, trans. Margritt A. Engel and O.W. Frost (Stanford: Stanford University Press, 1988).

Thevet, André, *The new found worlde, or Antactike [...]* (London: Henrie Bynneman, 1568; Ann Arbor: Text Creation Partnership, 2020). http://name.umdl.umich.edu/A13665.0001.001

ACKNOWLEDGEMENTS

Heartfelt thanks to the editors of the following journals in which some of these poems first appeared, some in earlier versions:

Cold Mountain Review: "*Glaucopsyche xerces*" and "*Hydrodamalis gigas*"

Portland Review: "*Melanoplus spretus*" and "*Nycticorax olsoni*"

Spillway: "*Vanvoorstia bennettiana*"

THINK: "*Cylindraspis vosmaeri,*" "*Picaea critchfieldii,*" and "*Tympanuchus cupido cupido*"

Zone 3: "*Mammut Americanum*" and "*Megaloceros giganteus*"

ABOUT THE AUTHOR

Nathan Manley is a writer and erstwhile English teacher from Loveland, Colorado. He holds a master's degree in English literature from the University of Northern Colorado. For now, he resides with his wife and two cats among the great deciduous forests of New England, where he is pursuing a JD at the University of New Hampshire. He is the author of one chapbook, *NUMINA LOCI* (Mighty Rogue Press, 2018). Recent poems have appeared or are forthcoming in *Portland Review, THINK, Natural Bridge, Crab Creek Review, Split Rock Review,* and others. His work has also been nominated for *Best of the Net.* You can find his writing and instrumental music at nathanmmanley.com.

Made in the USA
Middletown, DE
11 November 2021